OKLAHOMA

Past and Present

Robert L. Dorman, Ph.D.

rosen publishing's
rosen
central

New York

To my middle schooler, Adam

Published in 2011 by The Rosen Publishing Group, Inc.
29 East 21st Street, New York, NY 10010

First Edition

Library of Congress Cataloging-in-Publication Data

Dorman, Robert L.
Oklahoma: past and present / Robert L. Dorman. — 1st ed.
   p. cm. — (United States: past and present)
Includes bibliographical references and index.
ISBN 978-1-4358-9493-8 (library binding)
ISBN 978-1-4358-9520-1 (pbk.)
ISBN 978-1-4358-9554-6 (6-pack)
1. Oklahoma—Juvenile literature. I. Title.
F694.3.D67 2011
976.6—dc22

                                                      2010002591

Manufactured in Malaysia

CPSIA Compliance Information: Batch #S10YA: For further information, contact Rosen Publishing, New York, New York, at 1-800-237-9932.

On the cover: Top left: The 1919 Oklahoma Land Race. Top right: The Golden Driller statue in Tulsa. Bottom: A view of Oklahoma City's Bricktown Canal.

Contents

Oklahoma is a major producer of oil and natural gas. It's situated in the south-central region of the United States, known as the Great Plains. Because the land is mostly flat, Oklahoma is known for its severe weather, including frequent and violent tornadoes.

Introduction

Oklahoma has the slogan "Native America" printed on its license plates, highlighting the state's historic ties to Native American peoples. The word "Oklahoma" means "red people," and today there are thirty-eight official Indian tribes and nations living in Oklahoma. Yet "Native America" is also meant to suggest something else—the strong belief that Oklahomans share in what they see as the all-American values of hard work, family, personal responsibility, and religious faith.

Many people around the country only know about Oklahoma through its very successful college football teams. These teams are a source of great pride to Oklahomans and indicate the competitive spirit and endurance that helped build the state. In fact, a large part of Oklahoma was first settled during the 1890s by land runs, which were literally races run by people on foot, horseback, or in wagons to stake their claim to the best piece of land that they could find. The state's official nickname, the Sooner State, is taken from the sooners, who tried to cross the starting line "sooner" than other land-seekers.

Established in 1907, Oklahoma—one of the youngest states—experienced tragedy and hardship over the years. In every case, Oklahomans pulled together and rebuilt after their loss. The state motto sums up their spirit: "Labor Conquers All Things."

THE GEOGRAPHY OF OKLAHOMA

Oklahoma's landscape is very diverse, with twelve distinct environments or ecoregions. While the western part of Oklahoma has open plains, the eastern half is generally wooded or forested. From west to east, the state slopes lower in altitude, from 4,000 feet (1,219 meters) or more down to a few hundred feet above sea level. Oklahoma has several mountain ranges, and it has more than two thousand man-made lakes—more than any other state. Although famous for its tornadoes and violent weather, Oklahoma's climate is considered mild, with plenty of wind, sunshine, and an average annual temperature of 60 degrees Fahrenheit (15 degrees Celsius).

Oklahoma's Twelve Ecoregions

According to the U.S. Environmental Protection Agency (EPA), Oklahoma is one of the most environmentally diverse states in the Union. While many states have only four or five different ecoregions, Oklahoma has twelve, each with its own particular mix of landforms, climate, plants, and animals. These twelve ecoregions are the High Plains, Southwestern Tablelands, Central Great Plains, Flint Hills, Cross Timbers, East Central Texas Plains, South Central Plains,

A thunderstorm forms over the Central Great Plains eco-region in western Oklahoma. Annual precipitation in the state ranges from 16 inches (40 centimeters) in the Panhandle to 50 inches (127 cm) in the southeast.

Ouachita Mountains, Arkansas Valley, Boston Mountains, Ozark Highlands, and Central Irregular Plains.

Many of these ecoregions extend into neighboring states. But in Oklahoma, they come together to form a fascinating mosaic of different landscapes to experience. Along the Little River in the South Central Plains, for example, you can find cypress trees, swamps, and alligators. More than 500 miles (805 kilometers) away, in the Southwestern Tablelands at the western tip of the Panhandle, you might see piñon trees and bighorn sheep like those found in the Rocky Mountains.

In the Ouachita Mountains of southeastern Oklahoma, there are long ridges up to 2,500 feet (762 m) high covered with a great variety

The Arkansas River

People have been traveling up and down the Arkansas River for centuries. But in the past, it could often be a difficult trip. The level of water in the river might vary greatly, sometimes flooding and other times offering only a narrow stream in an empty riverbed. Even when there was sufficient water, snags of driftwood and other obstructions might block the way. In 1824, the steamboat *Florence* first reached Fort Gibson in what would later be eastern Oklahoma. By the 1840s and 1850s, regular steamboat traffic occurred between Fort Gibson and Fort Smith on the Arkansas border—that is, when the water was high enough.

The McClellan-Kerr Arkansas River Navigation System (MKARNS) has made a huge difference for river transportation. Completed in 1971 after nearly two decades of effort, the MKARNS was the most expensive public works project ever built by the U.S. Army Corps of Engineers at a cost of $1.2 billion. A channel 9 feet (3 m) deep and up to 250 feet (76 m) wide was dredged for 445 miles (716 km) from the Mississippi River to the Tulsa Port of Catoosa in Oklahoma. Eighteen locks and dams have been built in Oklahoma and Arkansas to raise and lower barges up and down the difference in elevation like stair steps, about 420 feet (128 m) total over the course of the river. The MKARNS provides landlocked Oklahoma with access to the sea.

Today, according to figures from the City of Tulsa-Rogers County Port Authority, more than a thousand barges regularly travel on the MKARNS each year, carrying an annual average of 13 million tons (11.8 million metric tons) of cargo. Fully loaded, each barge is capable of moving as much as 480 semitrailers. And if the barges ever have trouble, they can call for help from the U.S. Coast Guard, which now has a cutter on patrol in Oklahoma.

of hardwood and pine trees. The area is frequented by black bears, and trout fishing is available in some of its clear, cool streams. In the Cross Timbers, a large area of low wooded hills in the east-central part of the state, you will see the state's most common trees, post oak and blackjack oak. Farther on to the northwest, you might encounter flattopped buttes and mesas of bare red sandstone, along with occasional dry salt plains and gypsum caves—the Central Great Plains. Huge colonies of Mexican free-tailed bats live in some of the caverns, and grassy farmlands stretch as far as the eye can see.

Turner Falls, in the Arbuckle Mountains, is one of Oklahoma's most well-known natural attractions.

Mountains

Oklahoma has four principal mountainous areas: the Ozark Plateau and the Ouachita Mountains in the eastern part of the state, the Arbuckle Mountains in south-central Oklahoma, and the Wichita Mountains in the southwest. Geologically speaking, the Ouachitas, Arbuckles, and Wichitas are associated with the Appalachian mountain system of the eastern United States. They are among the oldest mountains in the country. Some granite formations in the Arbuckles date back 1.4 billion years.

Oklahoma's mountains are popular tourist destinations, especially attractions like Turner Falls in the Arbuckles, the highest waterfall in the state at 77 feet (23 m). In 1905, the Wichita Mountains were chosen to be the site of the first national preserve for the last few remaining bison, protecting them from extinction. Today, the herd numbers several hundred, free to roam thousands of acres in the Wichita Mountains Wildlife Refuge along with elk, deer, and longhorn cattle.

Oklahomans can enjoy many kinds of boating and sailing, thanks to the state's large number of man-made lakes, such as Lake Hefner in Oklahoma City.

Rivers and Lakes

Oklahoma's two main river basins are formed by the Arkansas River and the Red River. Both are major tributaries of the Mississippi River. There are other significant rivers in the state, including the Washita River, the Canadian River, and the Cimarron River. But the Arkansas and Red rivers drain wide areas and have been important historically in Oklahoma's development. The Red River, for example, forms the southern border of Oklahoma with Texas.

Oklahoma and Texas also share Lake Texoma, which is the second largest lake in the state, created when the Red River was dammed in 1944. The largest is Lake Eufaula, located in eastern Oklahoma. It measures 105,000 acres (42,492 hectares) and has more than 600 miles (965 km) of shoreline. The third largest lake, Grand Lake O' the Cherokees in northeastern Oklahoma, features Pensacola Dam, the world's longest multiple-arch dam at 6,100 feet (1,859 m) across.

Boating and fishing are very popular in Oklahoma, and on summer weekends, many Oklahomans may be heard to say that they are "going to the lake." Catfish, crappie, and bass, along with more exotic species like paddlefish, are caught in Oklahoma's rivers and lakes.

Violent Weather

Oklahoma lies at the heart of Tornado Alley, an area of the central United States where powerful tornadoes are frequent compared with the rest of the country. The

Storm chasers gather scientific data about tornadoes and capture dramatic images, like this one of a twister near Cordell in 1981.

state sees an average of sixty tornadoes each year. Many of them occur between April and June, when cold fronts moving southward clash with the warm, moist air coming north from the Gulf of Mexico.

Research at the National Severe Storms Laboratory in Norman has shown that south-central Oklahoma is the likeliest place on Earth for the most violent type of tornado to form. But all parts of the state have been struck by the storms. The tornado that hit the city of Woodward in 1947 was the deadliest in state history, killing 107 people. The 1999 tornado outbreak that ripped across the southern part of the Oklahoma City metropolitan area was the single costliest storm, at $1.2 billion. It damaged or destroyed almost eight thousand buildings and twenty thousand cars, and it left forty people dead. The fastest winds ever measured in a tornado—318 miles (499 km) per hour—happened during this storm.

Chapter 2

THE HISTORY OF OKLAHOMA

Oklahoma's prehistory extends back thousands of years, when bands of nomadic Paleo-Indians lived in the region and hunted bison and other game. In northwestern Oklahoma, archaeologists have discovered a piece of artwork created by these early people more than ten thousand years ago—a bison skull with a red lightning bolt painted on its forehead.

Much later, around 850 CE, the Caddoan people established a prosperous trading and religious center on the Arkansas River near what is now the town of Spiro in eastern Oklahoma. Thousands of artifacts have been unearthed from the Spiro Mounds and are now in museums around the world.

Since the Spanish conquistador Francisco Vásquez de Coronado first passed through the area in 1541, fourteen different flags have flown over all or parts of the region that became Oklahoma as different countries and states laid claim to its territory. These include the flags of Spain, Britain, France, Mexico, Texas, the Confederacy, and the United States.

Indian Removal

Although Plains tribes such as the Wichitas lived in Oklahoma long before the arrival of the Europeans, many Native American tribes

During the 1870s, Native American peoples throughout Indian Territory sent delegates to the Okmulgee Council, which attempted to establish an independent multitribal government.

were forced to move there from the eastern United States during the nineteenth century because of a government policy known as Indian removal. In exchange for their homelands in the East, tribes were given new lands in what became known as Indian Territory.

The most infamous example of Indian removal involved the so-called Five Civilized Tribes: the Choctaw, the Chickasaw, the Muscogee (Creek), the Cherokee, and the Seminole. During the 1820s and 1830s, thousands of men, women, and children were forced to abandon their homes in Georgia, Alabama, and other southern states to start over in the West. They suffered great hardship, hunger, and disease, and many of them died.

PAST AND PRESENT

The Cherokee Indians

The terrible ordeal of removing the Cherokee people from their Georgia homeland from 1838 to 1839 has come to be known as the Trail of Tears. Many were forced to live in internment camps before their trek westward to Indian Territory. An estimated 1,500 people died in the camps, and another 1,600 perished during the difficult, months-long journey. Even after their arrival in their new home in what is now eastern Oklahoma, more Cherokee fell to disease and starvation as they endured the hardship of rebuilding their way of life in a strange new place.

The Cherokee rebounded in a remarkably short period of time. By the 1840s and 1850s, their economy was prospering. Unfortunately, much of this progress was destroyed during the Civil War (1861–1865). In the 1890s and early 1900s, the Cherokee's independence was further undermined when the allotment process broke up their lands into individual homesteads, many of which were stolen from tribal members by unscrupulous whites.

Beginning in the 1930s, the tribe very gradually reasserted its right to govern itself. In 1975, a new constitution created a three-branch tribal government, headed by a principal chief. One of the first principal chiefs elected under the new constitution was a woman, Wilma Mankiller, who served from 1985 to 1995.

Today, the Cherokee Nation is one of the largest Native American tribes in the United States, with a population of more than three hundred thousand. The nation directly provides services to tribal members in a nonreservation area of more than 7,000 square miles (18,130 sq km) in eastern Oklahoma. The Cherokee also own numerous tribal businesses and industries. Overall, their future seems bright.

More than thirteen thousand Cherokees were forced to march 800 miles (1,287 km) on the Trail of Tears.

The removal of the Five Civilized Tribes was only the beginning of a process that eventually brought members of more than sixty tribes to Indian Territory. Yet by the 1880s, pressure mounted to open these lands to white settlement as well. A new policy known as allotment started in 1887; it began dividing up tribal domains into individual homesteads. The U.S. government broke its promise that the tribes subject to removal would have their new lands "for as long as the waters flow."

The Land Runs

During the 1880s, a movement known as the Boomers, led by David L. Payne, agitated for areas of Indian Territory to be opened to white settlement. On April 22, 1889, the Boomers at last got their wish when the Unassigned Lands in the central part of the territory became the site of the first land run. Nearly fifty thousand people lined up along the borders to race each other to stake a claim to a homestead or a town lot. Some settlers tried to sneak in before the noon starting time and became known as sooners.

In all, five land runs between 1889 and 1895 opened up millions of acres of what would become central and northwestern Oklahoma. The largest land run occurred in the Cherokee Outlet on September 16, 1893, when more than one hundred thousand people made the race.

Tulsa Race Riot

Although the state constitution and other laws deprived them of the right to vote and forced them into separate schools, some blacks were prospering in Oklahoma by the 1920s, particularly in oil boomtowns such as Tulsa. There, the Greenwood neighborhood had become known as the Black Wall Street, featuring many black-owned businesses, fine homes, and impressive churches.

Greenwood became the target of one of the worst race riots in U.S. history beginning on May 31, 1921, when a black teenager named Dick Rowland was arrested for the alleged assault of a white woman. After a white mob was thwarted in its desire to lynch Rowland, it turned its fury on the residents of Greenwood. Blacks were turned out of their homes by marauding whites and marched to internment centers. Hundreds of homes and businesses were looted and then burned to the ground. Machine guns and even an airplane were involved in the attack, which made prosperous Greenwood into a wasteland. The official death toll was thirty-nine. Later estimates put the number between 150 and 300 killed.

Oklahomans ignored this terrible event for decades. But in recent years, efforts have been made to heal the scars with a scholarship fund and a planned memorial to those who lost their lives.

The Dust Bowl

The demand for grain during World War I (1914–1918) prompted farmers to plow up large areas of the southern Great Plains, removing the natural grass cover that held the soil in place. When a prolonged drought hit in the 1930s, the resulting dust storms that occurred created a wind-eroded region known as the Dust Bowl that centered on the Oklahoma Panhandle.

The worst of these dust storms happened on April 14, 1935, a day known as Black Sunday. A strong cold front swept southward and carried winds of over 50 miles (80 km) per hour. What had been a clear sunny afternoon suddenly turned darker than night. People fled to their cellars or prayed in churches for the storm to end. Many animals and birds choked to death on dust, and a number of people died of "dust pneumonia."

A farmer and his sons run for shelter in Cimarron County, one of the areas hardest hit by dust storms during the Dust Bowl of the 1930s.

Many farmers abandoned the Panhandle in the 1930s, and some joined the Okie migration to California to search for better opportunities. In time, the rains did return, and the farmers who remained in the Panhandle learned to farm in ways that better conserved the soil.

The Oklahoma City Bombing

At 9:02 AM on April 19, 1995, a terrorist named Timothy McVeigh detonated a 4,800-pound (2,177 kilogram) truck bomb outside the Alfred P. Murrah Federal Building in downtown Oklahoma City. McVeigh and his accomplice, Terry Nichols, constructed the bomb using common fertilizer and fuel oil. It exploded with a force of more than two tons (two metric tons) of TNT.

Nine floors of the Murrah building collapsed in the massive explosion, as did ten nearby buildings, and twenty-five more structures

The empty chairs at the Oklahoma City National Memorial symbolize the loss of the 168 people who died in the terrorist attack on April 19, 1995.

were damaged. The human toll of the bombing was 168 killed—including 19 children—and 850 injured. The horror of the event was brought home to people around the world by the photograph of an Oklahoma City firefighter carrying the lifeless body of one of the young children.

A national memorial was dedicated on the site of the bombing in 2001. Special accommodations were made for an elm known as the Survivor Tree, which somehow had withstood the blast. Cuttings from the tree were planted all over America to symbolize hope and renewal in the face of the threat from terrorism.

Chapter 3

THE GOVERNMENT OF OKLAHOMA

Oklahoma is considered to be one of the more politically conservative states in the Union. For most of its history, the Democratic Party was the main party in the state. But in recent years, the Republicans have become more popular. Oklahoma was the first state to put term limits on its legislators. The annual legislative session lasts only ninety days. All tax increases at the state level must be approved by three-fourths of the state legislature or by a vote of the people. As can be seen, Oklahomans strongly believe in limited government.

Executive Branch

The governor of Oklahoma, like those of other states, is the head of the executive branch of government. The governor may serve no more than two four-year terms in office. He or she is advised by a cabinet of agency heads that includes the secretary of environment and the secretary of human services. The governor has the authority to veto bills submitted by the legislature and to call special emergency sessions of the legislature. In its history, Oklahoma has only elected three Republican governors. The other twenty-one governors have all been Democrats.

The Oklahoma legislature is sometimes called into special session beyond its regular session. Here, state senators are being sworn in for an impeachment trial.

Besides the governor, the executive branch includes other elected heads of individual state agencies and departments, such as the superintendent of public instruction, the attorney general, and the state treasurer.

Legislative Branch

Like many states, Oklahoma has a bicameral or two-chamber legislature. There are 101 members in the house of representatives and 48 members in the senate. Representatives serve two-year terms, and senators have their seats for four-year terms. But no legislator may hold his or her seat for more than twelve years because of term limits.

Each year, the legislature must pass a budget to fund state programs and agencies. Currently, education receives more than half of the state's annual budget, and other large appropriations go to health, human services, and corrections (prisons).

Judicial Branch

Oklahoma's legal system is different from many other states in that there are two highest courts, rather than one. The Oklahoma Court of Criminal Appeals hears criminal cases that have been appealed (that is, sent for review) from the lower courts. The Oklahoma

The Missing Capitol Dome: Then and Now

It took more than eighty years to finish building the state capitol of Oklahoma. When it was originally designed in 1914, it was supposed to have a large central dome much like the national capitol in Washington, D.C., or those found in other states. For most of Oklahoma's first century, however, its capitol was "hatless"—missing a dome.

Oklahoma City was not the first capital city of Oklahoma. That status went to the town of Guthrie, the territorial capital, which was supposed to continue as the state capital until 1913. But Oklahoma's first governor, Charles N. Haskell, and a group of Oklahoma City businessmen wanted the capital to move sooner. After a bitter fight and a special statewide ballot in 1910, Oklahoma City was chosen to be the new site by a wide margin. Overnight, Haskell had the official state seal driven down from Guthrie to the Oklahoma City hotel where he had set up the governor's office—identified with a hand-lettered sign.

Ground was broken for a new capitol building in 1914, with $1.5 million budgeted for its construction. By 1915, it was clear that this amount would not be enough to complete the construction with a full-sized dome. So a roof-hugging "saucer dome" was installed, as were columns that could support a larger dome in the future. The state government moved into the building in 1917.

There the issue largely remained until the year 2000, when Governor Frank Keating announced that a dome would at last be built to mark the upcoming state centennial in 2007. More than $20 million in private and public funds was raised, and the new dome was finally dedicated on statehood day in 2002—eighty-five years late.

Supreme Court considers appeals for civil cases, such as property disputes or broken contracts. The governor appoints the justices on these highest courts. But many judges for the lower courts in the state are elected outright, or voters choose to retain them after a certain period if they were appointed.

The next level below the supreme court is the intermediate court of civil appeals, one located in Tulsa and the other in Oklahoma City. At the local level, Oklahoma has twenty-six district courts, as well as elected district attorneys to bring cases to trial.

Local and County Government

Oklahoma has seventy-seven counties. Each county has a county seat, which is a large town or city where the county government is located. Two of the most important officials at the county level are the county sheriff and the county commissioner. County sheriffs and their deputies provide local law enforcement and operate county jails. County commissioners maintain local roads and bridges and oversee county government. During the early 1980s, Oklahoma's county commissioners were involved in one of the biggest political corruption scandals in American history. In the end, 165 commissioners from across the state were convicted of taking money or favors from road construction companies and others seeking to do business with their counties.

Tribal Governments

Driving down Oklahoma's highways, you will often see unusual license plates on other cars. These plates are issued by some of

In 2005, Native Americans celebrated the beginning of construction on the American Indian Cultural Center. State funding for the project recognized the significance of Native Americans in Oklahoma.

Oklahoma's tribal governments. Each of the state's thirty-eight federally recognized tribes has its own government. Many proudly refer to themselves as nations to emphasize their independence. Some tribal governments have their own executive, legislative, and judicial branches, including police forces. They may also provide health care and other programs for tribal members. And most operate a variety of tribally owned businesses. Although only one tribe, the Osage Nation, has its own reservation, Oklahoma's other tribes govern within "tribal jurisdictional areas" or "tribal statistical areas" that cover more than two-thirds of the state.

Chapter 4

THE ECONOMY OF OKLAHOMA

For much of its history, Oklahoma staked its prosperity on agriculture and oil production. Both of these industries, however, are subject to extreme ups and downs, depending on global supply and even the weather. In recent decades, the state's economy has matured and diversified, providing a more steady foundation for growth.

Manufacturing and Service Industries

Manufacturing has grown significantly in the state since World War II. Construction equipment, tires, plastics, food products, paper, electronics, household appliances, and aircraft components are just some of the manufactured goods produced in Oklahoma today.

Service industries form the largest sector of Oklahoma's economy. The Oklahoma Department of Commerce lists the retail giant Walmart as the top private employer in the state, with at least twenty-nine thousand employees. Hospitals and universities are also among the state's largest employers. Aircraft maintenance provides many high-paying jobs as well. Customer service centers for such industries as telecommunications, computers, and rental cars have been established in Oklahoma because of its friendly people and convenient location in the Central time zone.

Government Jobs

According to a 2008 Oklahoma Department of Commerce report, the single largest employer in Oklahoma—public or private—is the state government, with more than thirty-six thousand employees. The federal government, particularly the U.S. military, is also important to the state's economy. In fact, four of the top five largest employers in Oklahoma are government entities, including Tinker Air Force Base in Midwest City, Fort Sill in Lawton, and the U.S. Postal Service statewide.

The state government offers generous incentives to businesses to locate new facilities in Oklahoma, such as this customer service center for a major computer manufacturer.

Energy

The oil and natural gas industries still play a key role in Oklahoma's economy, more than a century after the Nellie Johnstone No. 1 became the state's first producing oil well in 1897.

According to the Mid-Continent Oil and Gas Association of Oklahoma, seventy-two out of the state's seventy-seven counties still have producing oil or gas wells. As of 2008, there were more than 120,000 oil and gas wells operating in the state, with an annual

The Cattle Industry

Native Americans were the first "cowboys" in Oklahoma. As early as the 1830s, tribes that had been removed to Indian Territory were raising cattle in their new home. Beginning in the 1840s, cattle were also being driven northward over the Shawnee Trail from Texas across Indian Territory to Missouri. After the Civil War, the cattle drives shifted westward to the Chisholm Trail, with its endpoint at Abilene, Kansas. Cowboys ushered along herds averaging 2,500 cattle for hundreds of miles, a trip that took weeks to complete. It was these cattle drives that were later made famous in western movies. An estimated five million cattle and one million horses were moved up the Chisholm Trail between 1867 and 1884.

The great cattle drives ended after the 1880s, but cowboys could still find plenty of work on the many large ranches that were established in Oklahoma, such as the 101 Ranch in the northern part of the state. Covering 135,000 acres (54,632 hectares) at its height, the 101 Ranch was so large that it had its own schools and post office.

Cattle raising continues to be a substantial element of Oklahoma's economy, especially in places such as Osage County, where cattle can graze on the rich bluestem grass of the tallgrass prairie. The Oklahoma National Stock Yards Company in Oklahoma City bills itself as the world's largest stocker and feeder cattle market, where up to half a million cattle are sold annually. According to the 2007 Census of Agriculture, there are more than five million cattle statewide, with annual sales of nearly $2 billion. Many of these animals are concentrated in giant feedlots in the Panhandle, where they are shipped to be fattened on corn before slaughter. A single such operation can feed more than fifty thousand cattle at a time. It is very different from the days when longhorns and cowboys ambled up the Chisholm Trail.

production of 66 million barrels of oil and 1.6 trillion cubic feet (45.3 cubic meters) of natural gas. Oklahoma ranked fifth in the nation for oil output and third nationally for natural gas.

Since 2000, the potential for wind energy has gained a lot of attention in Oklahoma, with developers hoping to tap the high prevailing winds, especially in the western third of the state. A report by the Oklahoma Wind Power Initiative showed that there were eight wind farms in Oklahoma, generating enough electricity to power more than two hundred thousand homes.

Oklahoma has the eighth highest annual wind energy potential in the United States. Each one of these typical wind turbines generates 1.5 megawatts of electricity.

Agriculture and Forestry

Even though more than half of its residents live in metropolitan areas, Oklahoma has the image of a rural state—and with good reason. Agriculture remains an important part of the state's economy. The 2007 Census of Agriculture shows that there are more than eighty-six thousand farms in Oklahoma, covering 35 million acres

Since 2000, casino-style gambling has rapidly grown into a billion-dollar industry in Oklahoma. This Cherokee casino is one of dozens owned and operated by the state's Indian tribes.

(14.2 million ha). Livestock raising is the largest sector of the farm economy, with annual sales of cattle, hogs, and poultry totaling more than $5 billion. As of 2007, Oklahoma ranked as one of the country's top ten biggest producers of cattle, hogs, horses, and poultry.

Wheat is the state's most widely grown food grain, but a variety of other crops may also be found on Oklahoma's farms. Corn, sorghum, oats, and alfalfa hay are grown particularly to provide feed for live-stock raisers and large-scale feedlots. Rye, soybeans, cotton, and peanuts add further value and diversity to the state's crop production, which totals nearly $2 billion annually.

Timber is another valuable "crop" in Oklahoma. The Oklahoma Forestry Services agency reports that Oklahoma's 10 million acres (4 million ha) of forests contribute $2 billion to the economy each year.

Gaming Industry

By far the fastest-growing portion of Oklahoma's economy in recent years has been the gaming industry. According to 2008 industry reports published in the *Oklahoman*, there were nearly one hundred casinos and other gaming operations in the state as of that year, with annual revenues of almost $2 billion. The number of slot machines in Oklahoma is behind only California (which has more than ten times Oklahoma's population) and Nevada, home to the gambling capital of Las Vegas. Oklahoma's tribal governments are the sole operators of the state's casino-style gaming industry. There is also a statewide lottery run by the state government with annual revenues of over $200 million.

PEOPLE FROM OKLAHOMA:
PAST AND PRESENT

Oklahoma's people are diverse, just like its landscape. Nearly 10 percent of all Native Americans in the United States live in Oklahoma. Czechs, Germans, Russians, and other European immigrants settled in Oklahoma during the frontier era, as did African Americans from the South. Recently, Hispanics have become the most rapidly growing minority in the state. And Asian immigrants, especially the Vietnamese, have founded vibrant communities there. Oklahoma also has had its share of true individuals.

Garth Brooks (1962–) Country singer Garth Brooks, the biggest-selling solo recording artist in American history, was born in Tulsa and grew up in Yukon, Oklahoma. His phenomenally successful album, *No Fences* (1990), sold more than sixteen million copies and garnered numerous awards. Brooks's 1998 live album, *Double Live*, is the biggest-selling live album in history. Altogether, Brooks has sold 128 million albums, the most for a solo artist and second only to the Beatles, according to the Recording Industry Association of America.

Angie Debo (1890–1988) Angie Debo moved from Kansas to Marshall, Oklahoma Territory, in her parents' covered

Ralph Ellison is pictured here in 1957 while at the American Academy in Rome, where he worked on his second novel as well as an essay about his early life in Oklahoma City.

wagon. She was a pioneering historian of Native Americans who wrote a number of books about Oklahoma, including her most famous work, *And Still the Waters Run: The Betrayal of the Five Civilized Tribes* (1940). The book uncovered the shameful story of how Native Americans were cheated out of their lands during Oklahoma's early years.

Ralph Ellison (1914–1994) Internationally renowned novelist Ralph Ellison was born in Oklahoma City and grew up in the city's Deep Deuce neighborhood. For most of his career, Ellison lived in Manhattan, but he always saw himself as an Oklahoman. He was the author of the novel *Invisible Man* (1952), which won the National Book Award and is regarded

Will Rogers

Will Rogers was one of the first multimedia superstars. Born in 1879 near Oologah, Indian Territory, Rogers was a Cherokee Indian who spent his youth as a cowboy on his family's ranch. His first big success in show business came as a live performer on Broadway with the Ziegfeld Follies. He astounded audiences with his rope tricks, including one in which he threw three separate lassos around a horse and its rider at the same time. Rogers's onstage jokes and witty sayings were equally entertaining, and by the 1920s, he was being offered Hollywood movie roles. He eventually starred in more than sixty movies, both silent and sound.

Besides his stage and screen work, Rogers wrote a newspaper column that appeared in more than six hundred newspapers nationwide and was read regularly by millions. Beginning in 1930, he also had a weekly radio show that was one of the most popular on the air. Rogers's jokes about politics shaped national opinion in the way that late-night TV comedians do today. His humor helped ease the misery that people suffered during the years of the Great Depression.

Will Rogers was at the height of his popularity when he died tragically in a plane crash in 1935. The whole country mourned his loss. He was buried in a tomb at what is now the Will Rogers Memorial in Claremore, Oklahoma.

Rogers lived on in later decades through the actor James Whitmore's popular stage impersonation as well as the Tony Award–winning musical *The Will Rogers Follies*.

The beloved humorist Will Rogers is remembered for famous sayings such as "I never met a man I didn't like."

as one of the major literary masterpieces of the twentieth century. It challenged the prevalent racism of the era.

Woody Guthrie (1912–1967) Woody Guthrie was a world-famous folk singer who was born and raised in Okemah, Oklahoma. He wrote "This Land Is Your Land" (1940) and a number of other classic songs based on his experiences among poor rural people in the West during the Great Depression. His autobiography, *Bound for Glory* (1943), is also considered a classic. He influenced many later recording artists, including singer-songwriter Bob Dylan.

Clara Luper (1923–) Civil rights activist Clara Luper, born in Okfuskee County, led the effort to end racial segregation at public places in Oklahoma. She is credited with staging one of the first sit-ins in the country in 1958, when she brought a group of black teenagers to an Oklahoma City drugstore and demanded service at the "whites-only" lunch counter. Businesses began to stop the practice because of the bad publicity.

Shannon Miller (1977–) Shannon Miller, from Edmond, Oklahoma, is the most decorated gymnast in U.S. history. During her career, she won nine world championship medals, including five gold, and a total of seven Olympic medals: two gold, two silver, and three bronze. Miller was the all-around world champion in women's gymnastics in 1993 and 1994. At the 1996 Olympic Games in Atlanta, Georgia, she shared in the team gold medal, and she became the first American ever to win a gold medal on the balance beam.

Shannon Miller is shown here competing at the 1993 World Championships, where she won the all-around gold medal. She repeated the feat in 1994.

William H. Murray (1869–1956) William H. "Alfalfa Bill" Murray, born in Toadsuck, Texas, was the most colorful politician in state history. During his career, the Democrat from Tishomingo served as house speaker (1907–1908), congressman (1913–1917), and governor (1931–1935). In the 1920s, Murray led an unsuccessful attempt to establish a colony of American farmers in Bolivia, South America. As governor, Murray became famous for antics such as nearly starting a war with the state of Texas over toll bridges. He was also known to be deeply prejudiced against blacks and Jews.

Thomas P. Stafford (1930–) Born in Weatherford, Oklahoma, Lieutenant General Thomas P. Stafford is the most distinguished of the many astronauts who have come from Oklahoma. He flew on two of NASA's Gemini missions (VI and IX), and he was commander of *Apollo 10* in 1969, during which he and his crew orbited the moon and descended in the lunar module to a few miles above the surface. Stafford also commanded the American spacecraft for the Apollo-Soyuz joint mission with the Soviet Union in 1975.

Jim Thorpe (1887–1953) Jim Thorpe, a member of the Sac and Fox tribe, was born near Prague, Indian Territory. He was called the greatest athlete in the world by the king of Sweden after winning both the decathlon and the pentathlon in the 1912 Olympic Games. His gold medals were taken away after it was revealed that he had played sports professionally before the games, which were then for amateurs only. The medals were reinstated decades later, after his death.

Thomas P. Stafford (*right*) and the crew of the *Apollo 10* are pictured prior to launch in 1969. Their spaceflight reached the fastest speed ever experienced by humans, 24,791 miles (39,897 km) per hour.

Bud Wilkinson (1916–1994) Although he was born in Minnesota, head coach Bud Wilkinson will forever be identified with the success of the University of Oklahoma football team. The Sooners won three national championships under his coaching (1950, 1955, and 1956). Above all, Wilkinson's teams will be remembered for their record forty-seven-game winning streak, which began in 1953 and lasted until 1957. The record has never been broken.

Timeline

12,000 + years ago Paleo-Indians live and hunt in the region that will become Oklahoma.

850 Caddoan Mound Builders establish a village at the site of the Spiro Mounds.

1541 Spanish conquistador Francisco Vásquez de Coronado visits the area.

1838 The Cherokee embark on the Trail of Tears.

1866 Post–Civil War treaties force the Five Civilized Tribes to give up millions of acres of land.

1868 General George A. Custer and the Seventh Cavalry massacre a Southern Cheyenne village in the Battle of the Washita.

1889 The first land run occurs on the Unassigned Lands.

1890 Oklahoma Territory is declared.

1897 The first commercial oil well, Nellie Johnstone No. 1, pumps oil.

1907 Oklahoma becomes the forty-sixth state in the Union.

1921 The Tulsa Race Riot results in at least thirty-nine deaths.

1930–1939 The Okies migrate to California.

1932–1939 The Dust Bowl hits Oklahoma.

1947 A tornado in Woodward kills 107 people.

1958 One of the nation's first sit-ins is staged in Oklahoma City to protest racial segregation.

1995 The Oklahoma City bombing, the worst act of domestic terrorism, kills 168 and injures 850.

1999 On May 3, a tornado outbreak in central Oklahoma causes $1.2 billion in damage and kills forty people.

2000 The University of Oklahoma Sooners football team wins their seventh national championship.

2008 The state's first major league sports franchise, the NBA Thunder, moves to Oklahoma City.

State motto:	*Labor Omnia Vincit* ("Labor Conquers All Things")
State capital:	Oklahoma City
State tree:	Redbud
State bird:	Scissor-tailed flycatcher
State flower:	Oklahoma rose
State fruit:	Strawberry
Statehood date and number:	November 16, 1907; forty-sixth state
State nickname:	The Sooner State
Total area and U.S. rank:	69,898 square miles (181,036 sq km); twentieth largest state
Population:	3,617,000
Highest elevation:	Black Mesa, at 4,973 feet (1,517 m)
Lowest elevation:	Little River, at 287 feet (88 m)

State flag

State seal

Major rivers:	Arkansas River, Red River, Canadian River, Cimarron River, Washita River
Major lakes:	Lake Eufaula, Lake Texoma, Grand Lake O' the Cherokees
Hottest recorded temperature:	120°F (49°C) at Alva, July 18, 1936
Coldest recorded temperature:	-27°F (-33°C) at Vinita, February 15, 1905
Origin of state name:	The word "Oklahoma" means "red people" in the Choctaw language
Chief agricultural products:	Cattle, hogs, poultry, timber, wheat, sorghum, rye, cotton, corn, soybeans, alfalfa
Major industries:	Oil, natural gas, construction equipment, tires, food products, household appliances, plastics, paper, electronics, aircraft components

Scissor-tailed flycatcher

Oklahoma rose

allotment An individual homestead or landholding.

amateur Describing nonprofessional participation in a sport or pastime.

appeal To request the review of the verdict or procedure of a legal trial.

appropriations Funds approved by legislatures to operate particular programs or agencies.

bicameral Having two legislative houses or chambers.

Boomer A promoter of white settlement in Indian Territory during the 1880s.

conquistador A sixteenth-century Spanish explorer and conqueror in the Americas.

cutter A boat in government service, such as those in the U.S. Coast Guard.

dredge To deepen the bed of a waterway with an earth-moving machine.

ecoregion An area of land that has a distinct ecosystem or environment.

impeachment Charges against a public official for crimes or misconduct in office.

internment Confinement or imprisonment.

jurisdictional Related to the area where a government may legally exercise its authority.

landform A type of physical feature on Earth's surface.

lasso A knotted loop of rope used to catch and secure livestock.

lynch To illegally hang or execute an individual, usually by the action of a mob.

Okie A jobless person from Oklahoma who migrated to the West during the Great Depression.

segregation The legalized separation of African Americans in schools and other public places during the twentieth century.

sit-in An organized demonstration in which participants seat themselves in an appropriate place and refuse to move as an act of protest.

sooner A person who tried to claim a homestead before the official start of the 1889 land run.

veto The rejection of new legislation by a governor or president.

Native American Cultural and Educational Authority (NACEA)

900 N. Broadway, Suite 200

Oklahoma City, OK 73102

(405) 239-5500

Web site: http://www.aiccm.org

The NACEA is a state agency that is constructing the American Indian Cultural Center and Museum in Oklahoma City to promote awareness and understanding of Oklahoma's Native American peoples.

Oklahoma Archaeological Survey

111 E. Chesapeake

Norman, OK 73019-5111

(405) 325-7211

Web site: http://www.ou.edu/cas/archsur/home.htm

Based at the University of Oklahoma, the Oklahoma Archaeological Survey studies and preserves Oklahoma's rich archaeological heritage.

Oklahoma Department of Libraries (ODL)

200 N.E. 18th Street

Oklahoma City, OK 73105

(800) 522-8116

Web site: http://www.odl.state.ok.us

The ODL is the state library of Oklahoma and the archives of the state government. It coordinates programs and resources with libraries across Oklahoma.

Oklahoma Department of Wildlife Conservation (ODWC)

1801 N. Lincoln Boulevard

Oklahoma City, OK 73105

(405) 521-3855

Web site: http://www.wildlifedepartment.com

The ODWC is a state agency that manages fish, game, and wildlife throughout Oklahoma. It also publishes a popular magazine, *Outdoor Oklahoma*.

Oklahoma Heritage Association

Gaylord-Pickens Oklahoma Heritage Museum
1400 Classen Drive
Oklahoma City, OK 73106
(405) 235-4458
Web site: http://oklahomaheritage.com
This nonprofit organization honors individual Oklahomans for their contributions to the state through the Oklahoma Hall of Fame and exhibits at the Gaylord-Pickens Museum.

Oklahoma Historical Society

2401 N. Laird Avenue
Oklahoma City, OK 73105
(405) 521-2491
Web site: http://www.okhistory.org
The Oklahoma Historical Society is a state agency that operates the Oklahoma History Center in Oklahoma City and a number of other important museums and historic sites statewide.

Oklahoma Tourism and Recreation Department

Travel and Tourism Division
120 N. Robinson Avenue, 6th Floor
P.O. Box 52002
Oklahoma City, OK 73152-2002
(800) 652-6552
Web site: http://www.travelok.com
This state agency promotes tourism in Oklahoma and provides information for travel planning.

Sam Noble Oklahoma Museum of Natural History (SNOMNH)

2401 Chautauqua Avenue
Norman, OK 73072-7029
(405) 325-4712

Web site: http://www.snomnh.ou.edu

One of the largest university-based natural history museums in the country, the SNOMNH has collections and exhibits related to Oklahoma's flora, fauna, and cultures, both modern and prehistoric.

Western History Collections

Monnet Hall

630 Parrington Oval, Room 452

Norman, OK 73019

(405) 325-3641

Web site: http://libraries.ou.edu/locations/?id=22

This is a special library and archive of the University of Oklahoma Libraries, with hundreds of thousands of books, photographs, and documents related to Oklahoma history, including many online digital collections.

Web Sites

Due to the changing nature of Internet links, Rosen Publishing has developed an online list of Web sites related to the subject of this book. This site is updated regularly. Please use this link to access the list:

http://www.rosenlinks.com/uspp/okpp

Baird, W. David, and Danney Goble. *The Story of Oklahoma*. 2nd ed. Norman, OK: University of Oklahoma Press, 2007.

Clark, Blue. *Indian Tribes of Oklahoma: A Guide*. Norman, OK: University of Oklahoma Press, 2009.

Dorman, Robert L. *It Happened in Oklahoma*. Guilford, CT: TwoDot, 2006.

Gilbert, Claudette Marie, and Robert L. Brooks. *From Mounds to Mammoths: A Field Guide to Oklahoma Prehistory*. 2nd ed. Norman, OK: University of Oklahoma Press, 2000.

Goins, Charles Robert, and Danney Goble. *Historical Atlas of Oklahoma*. 4th ed. Norman, OK: University of Oklahoma Press, 2006.

Keith, Harold. *Forty-Seven Straight: The Wilkinson Era at Oklahoma*. Norman, OK: University of Oklahoma Press, 1984.

Morgan, David R., Robert E. England, and George G. Humphreys. *Oklahoma Politics & Policies: Governing the Sooner State*. Lincoln, NE: University of Nebraska Press, 1991.

Palmer, Barbara. *Oklahoma: Off the Beaten Path*. 4th ed. Guilford, CT: Globe Pequot Press, 2003.

Ross, Glen. *On Coon Mountain: Scenes from a Childhood in the Oklahoma Hills*. Norman, OK: University of Oklahoma Press, 1992.

Schwarz, Melissa. *Wilma Mankiller: Principal Chief of the Cherokees*. New York, NY: Chelsea House, 1994.

Stallings, Frank L., Jr. *Black Sunday: The Great Dust Storm of April 14, 1935*. Austin, TX: Eakin Press, 2001.

BIBLIOGRAPHY

Armstrong, Connie G., ed. *Oklahoma Almanac, 2009–2010*. 52nd ed. Oklahoma City, OK: Oklahoma Department of Libraries, 2009.

Bement, Leland C. *Bison Hunting at Cooper Site: Where Lightning Bolts Drew Thundering Herds*. Norman, OK: University of Oklahoma Press, 1999.

Bryant, Keith L., Jr. *Alfalfa Bill Murray*. Norman, OK: University of Oklahoma Press, 1968.

Cherokee Nation. "A Brief History of the Cherokee Nation." 2000–2009. Retrieved October 17, 2009 (http://www.cherokee.org/Culture/57/Page/default.aspx).

City of Tulsa–Rogers County Port Authority. "Tulsa Port of Catoosa." Retrieved August 16, 2009 (http://www.tulsaport.com/index.htm).

Denson, Andrew. *Demanding the Cherokee Nation: Indian Autonomy and American Culture, 1830–1900*. Lincoln, NB: University of Nebraska Press, 2004.

Frankfurt-Short-Bruza Architects. "Oklahoma State Capitol Dome." Retrieved October 18, 2009 (http://www.oklahomadome.com/home2.htm).

Hirsch, James S. *Riot and Remembrance: The Tulsa Race War and Its Legacy*. Boston, MA: Houghton Mifflin, 2002.

Jackson, Lawrence. *Ralph Ellison: Emergence of Genius*. New York, NY: John Wiley & Sons, 2002.

Joyce, Davis G., ed. *"An Oklahoma I Had Never Seen Before": Alternative Views of Oklahoma History*. Norman, OK: University of Oklahoma Press, 1994.

Lyndon B. Johnson Space Center. "Thomas P. Stafford." 2004. Retrieved October 10, 2009 (http://www.jsc.nasa.gov/Bios/htmlbios/stafford-tp.html).

McLoughlin, William G. *After the Trail of Tears: The Cherokees' Struggle for Sovereignty, 1839–1880*. Chapel Hill, NC: University of North Carolina Press, 1993.

Mid-Continent Oil and Gas Association. "Oklahoma Oil and Gas Facts." 2009. Retrieved August 8, 2009 (http://www.okmoga.com/html/facts.php#drill).

Official Garth Brooks Web site. "Biography." 2006. Retrieved October 10, 2009 (http://www.Garthbrooks.com).

Oklahoma Department of Commerce. "Data and Research." 2009. Retrieved October 17, 2009 (http://www.okcommerce.gov).

Oklahoma Historical Society. "Encyclopedia of Oklahoma History and Culture." Retrieved August 8, 2009 (http://digital.library.okstate.edu/encyclopedia).

Oklahoma Tourism and Recreation Department. *9:02 A.M., April 19, 1995: The Official Record of the Oklahoma City Bombing*. Oklahoma City, OK: The Department, 2005.

Settle, William A. *The Dawning: A New Day for the Southwest: A History of the Tulsa District Corps of Engineers, 1939–1971*. Tulsa, OK: The District, 1975.

Shannon Miller Online. "Shannon Miller Biography." 2007–2009. Retrieved October 10, 2009 (http://shannonmiller.com/shannon-miller.php).

Stogsdill, Sheila. "Rapid Growth of Tribal Casinos Now Paying Off." *Oklahoman*, April 20, 2008. Retrieved October 10, 2009 (http://newsok.com/article/3230470/1208610830).

Thornton, Russell. *The Cherokees: A Population History*. Lincoln, NE: University of Nebraska Press, 1990.

U.S. Census Bureau. *Statistical Abstract of the United States: 2009*. Washington, DC: Government Printing Office, 2008.

U.S. Department of Agriculture. "The Census of Agriculture." 2009. Retrieved August 8, 2009 (http://www.agcensus.usda.gov).

Will Rogers Memorial Museums. "Will Rogers Biography." 2009. Retrieved August 16, 2009 (http://www.willrogers.com/willrogers/biography/will/will.html).

Woods, A. J., et al. *Ecoregions of Oklahoma*. Reston, VA: U.S. Geological Survey, 2005. Retrieved August 16, 2009 (http://www.epa.gov/wed/pages/ecoregions/ok_eco.htm).

Woody Guthrie Foundation. "Woody Guthrie—Biography." 2000–2009. Retrieved October 17, 2009 (http://www.woodyguthrie.org/biography/biography1.htm).

Worster, Donald. *Dust Bowl: The Southern Plains in the 1930s*. New York: Oxford University Press, 1982.

INDEX

A

agriculture and forestry, 27–29
Arkansas River, 8, 10, 12

B

Brooks, Garth, 30

C

cattle industry, 26, 29
Cherokee, 13, 14, 32
climate/weather, 6, 11
Coronado, Francisco Vásquez de, 12

D

Debo, Angie, 30–31
Dust Bowl, 16–17

E

ecoregions, 6–9
Ellison, Ralph, 31–33
energy industry, 25–27
executive branch of government, 19–20

G

gaming industry, 29
government jobs, 25
Guthrie, Woody, 33

J

judicial branch of government, 20–22

L

land runs, 5, 15
legislative branch of government, 20
local and county government, 22
Luper, Clara, 33

M

manufacturing and service industries, 24
McClellan-Kerr Arkansas River Navigation System (MKARNS), 8
Miller, Shannon, 33
mountains, 6, 7–9, 9–10
Murray, William H., 35

N

Native Americans, 5, 12–15, 26, 30,31, 32

O

Oklahoma City bombing, 17–18

P

Pensacola Dam, 10

R

rivers and lakes, 6, 10–11
Rogers, Will, 32

S

Spiro Mounds, 12
Stafford, Thomas P., 35

T

Thorpe, Jim, 35
tornadoes, 6, 11
Trail of Tears, 14
tribal governments, 22–23, 29
Tulsa Race Riot, 15–16
Turner Falls, 9–10

W

Wilkinson, Bud, 36

About the Author

Robert L. Dorman is a monographs librarian and associate professor of library science at Oklahoma City University. He holds a B.A. in history from the University of Oklahoma, an M.S. in library and information science from the Catholic University of America, and an M.A. and Ph.D. in history from Brown University. He is the author of three other books, including *It Happened in Oklahoma* (2006). He first became interested in Oklahoma history while in college after learning about his great-grandfather's career as a frontiersman. Hubert Dorman (1859–1918) lived among the Kickapoo Indians and other tribes while working as a government interpreter in the years before the 1889 land run. He participated in the land run and a few years later helped found Jones, Oklahoma, Robert's hometown near Oklahoma City.

Photo Credits